THE
GHOSTLY TALES
OF

LAKE
TAHOE

Published by Arcadia Children's Books
A Division of Arcadia Publishing
Charleston, SC
www.arcadiapublishing.com

First published 2023

Manufactured in the United States

ISBN 978-1-4671-9723-6

Library of Congress Control Number: 2023931836

All images courtesy of Shutterstock.com; p. 64 Jessica Bauman/Shutterstock.com; p. 80 Matt Gush/Shutterstock.com.

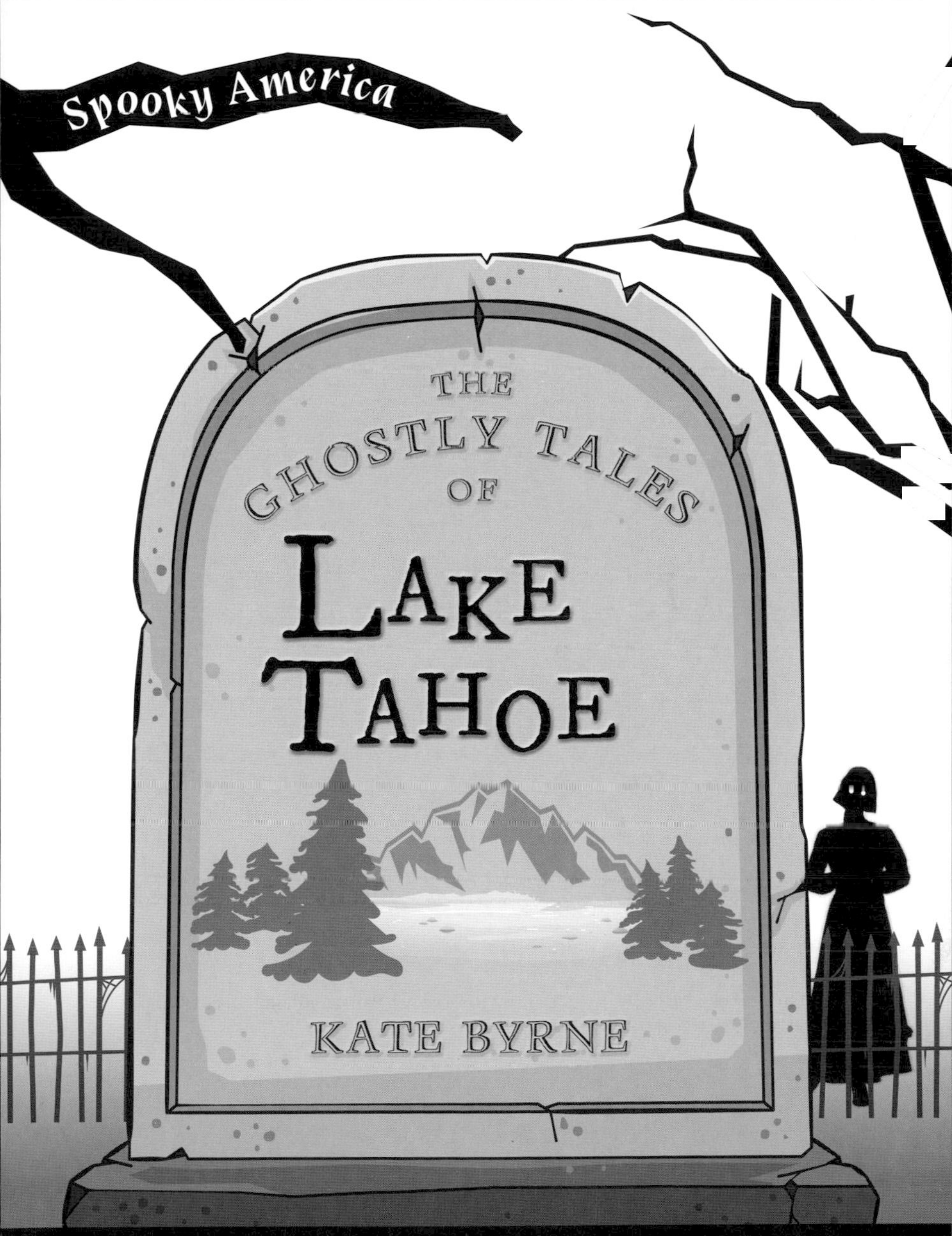

Adapted from *Haunted Lake Tahoe* by Janice Oberding

Oregon
Idaho
California
Nevada
Utah
Arizona
Lake Tahoe
1
2
3
4
5
6
7
8
9
10
11
12
13
14
15

Table of Contents & Map Key

Welcome to Spooky Lake Tahoe!

Looking through the pine trees, you can see the sun sparkling on the rippling waters of Lake Tahoe. A snow-capped mountain peak rises in the background of this dream vacation spot that has been called the Jewel of the Sierras and the Ocean in the Sky. It's special in so many ways. Its water is so clean, it's almost as pure as drinking water. Nestling the borders of California and Nevada, the lake is so large (it's the largest freshwater lake in the Sierra Nevada Mountains) that its shores are patrolled by the U.S. Coast Guard. It's so deep that if you were to dump the whole thing out, it would cover the whole state of California in fourteen inches of water! It's also ancient—nearly *two million* years old. Given its age, is it any surprise that Lake Tahoe is very haunted?

That's right—lurking beneath Tahoe's deep waters and around its hidden coves and bays, there are countless spirits, both friendly and frightening, who've chosen this beautiful place to spend eternity. Some haunt the hallways of the area's many hotels and casinos. Some can be found along the lake's rocky shores, showing up on misty mornings and ink-black evenings. There are even ghosts on the side of the twisty-turny roads winding through the rugged landscape. Locals believe Lake Tahoe might even have its very own lake monster! (Yup, just like the famous one in Loch Ness, Scotland.) After all, with water that deep . . . who KNOWS what sort of spooky secrets Tahoe might hold?

But it's not only the lake that's teeming with spooks—you may need to scan the skies as well. Tahoe is said to be the ancestral home to a mysterious bird called the Ong. This giant creature—rumored to have wings as tall as trees, giant webbed feet, a body covered in both feathers and scales, and a terrifying, human-like face—frightened the local Washoe people for ages. Could it still be hiding nearby today?

Despite ghosts and ghouls and monsters (oh my!), Tahoe remains an extremely popular holiday paradise. Lots of visitors means *lots* of local hotels. And lots of local hotels means even more . . . *HAUNTINGS*! In fact, there are so many hotel ghosts in and around Lake Tahoe, it would be a surprise if the hotel you stay at *didn't* have one. And if you think you can outsmart the ghosts by staying in a neighboring town, think again! The hauntings and strange happenings don't stop when you leave the lake.

Take Truckee, for example. This Wild West California town was once home to rowdy outlaws, crooked criminals, and the hardened lawmen who tried to stop them. Those disorderly days may have been long, *long* ago, but their legends still live on today in the form of ghosts. From rebels to robbers to gun-slinging gangsters—they haunt the

Old Truckee Jail and have been seen in the old Capitol building, too. There's even a haunted vacation home in Truckee. Is that a place *you'd* like to spend your summer break?

Read on to discover the spooky, creepy, ghostly stories you need to know about the Lake Tahoe area. Maybe you already believe in ghosts. Maybe you don't. But can you be so sure? You may have to visit one of America's most stunning (and stunningly spooky!) vacation destinations to find out for yourself.

The Mythical Beasts of Tahoe

You've probably heard of the Loch Ness monster—a prehistoric beast who, according to legend, lives at the bottom of Scotland's Loch Ness. ("Loch" is the Scottish, Gaelic, and Irish word for "lake.") Through the years, there have been many sightings of "Nessie," as many affectionately call the beast. But what does Nessie look like? And is she real . . . or just a myth?

Those who claim to have seen Nessie describe a long body that dives and flits beneath the lake. Its long fins slice the water. Its small head surfaces every so often to reveal a dragon-like neck covered in smooth, reptilian skin. Through the years, people have taken photographs of *something* coming out of the water. They claim it's the monster of Loch Ness. At the very least, it certainly looks like it could be an ancient creature.

But Loch Ness isn't the only lake that might have a monster. Lakes all around the world have been said to harbor ancient creatures—especially deep, dark lakes like Tahoe. In fact, Lake Tahoe is *so* deep (deeper than the Empire State building is tall!) that practically anything could be hiding down there undiscovered. Even . . . a mythical water beast.

Which brings us to *Tahoe Tessie*: the beastlike creature rumored to be hiding below the shimmering surface of Lake Tahoe. Going back more than one hundred years, the local Washoe and Paiute peoples have told the story of an underground tunnel beneath Cave Rock on the Nevada side of the lake. This is the place where many believe Tahoe Tessie lives. On those rare occasions when people claim to see her, they describe Tessie as a sea serpent. But . . . how would a *sea serpent* have ended up in a LAKE? Maybe the creature got lost somehow? Or maybe it's been there all along, hiding out since ancient times. The lake is two million years old, after all.

Like the Loch Ness Monster, some people think Tahoe Tessie is made up. They say Tessie is just "a big fish," which certainly seems more likely. And there are species of freshwater fish that can grow to be huge, like the white sturgeon or the alligator gar. But . . . can they grow big enough to be mistaken for a sea monster?

That is the question.

Now, there is some controversy and disbelief surrounding Tahoe Tessie. Some wonder if maybe the local authorities keep Tessie sightings secret because they don't want to scare away tourists. Others say Tessie is just a story created by local tourism authorities to attract visitors.

What do you think? Would you visit Cave Rock to try to see Tessie? Or would you avoid it?

Remember, Tessie is not the only strange creature people have spotted around Tahoe. To see the other creature, however, you'll have to look up from the lake. But be careful: The Washoe people have long spoken of this

winged creature that rises from the water, soars through the sky, and terrorizes people on the ground. It's called the Ong.

Some have described the Ong as a prehistoric bird. But could such a creature really exist? Those who have reported seeing it knew it to be larger than life. It was said to have the body of an eagle, webbed feet, and wings as long as the tallest pine trees. But its most horrifying feature was its face: it was almost human, but covered in hard scales.

Yikes!

Its frightful appearance was nothing compared to its behavior. The Ong had a nest submerged in the lake for a terrible reason: The Washoe people said it would collect drowning victims and bring them to the nest to eat them. It also hunted people who were alone or vulnerable. The Ong was said to even target children who were alone on the shore!

This terrible creature was almost impossible to kill. Its feathers were so dense they couldn't be penetrated with an arrow. Its scales protected its face and legs. However, the Ong had a weakness: it had no beak or claws.

The Washoe have a famous story about the Ong. It's also the story of how Lake Tahoe got its name. It all started one autumn, when hunting season was just coming to an end. It was the time when the semi-nomadic people who lived on the slopes of the mountains would move toward the valleys before the winter snows arrived.

A young Washoe woman had just turned sixteen. She was at the age when most women got married. Since her father was the chief, it was the custom that she marry the bravest man in the community. There was a man who many believed to be the bravest, but he was much older. And besides, she was in love with another: his name was Tahoe.

Tahoe loved her, too. But it seemed there was no way for them to be together. The young man was so distressed, he prayed to be taken by the Ong. Not long after he expressed his wishes to the Great Spirit, Tahoe saw the terrible Ong rising out of the water. He tried to get the creature's attention by jumping up and down. It worked. The Ong swooped down, caught Tahoe in his webbed feet, and carried him away.

Nearby, the rest of the community watched in horror as the creature disappeared over the forest toward the mountains with poor Tahoe hanging in its grasp. The Ong had a habit of dropping its victims into the lake from a great height so that they would sink right into its nest. But by the time Tahoe was truly in the clutches of the creature, he realized he didn't want to die after all.

He wrapped a buckskin cord around his waist and attached it to the Ong's leg. This took the creature by surprise. When it tried to drop him into the water, Tahoe didn't fall. The creature went wild. It lashed at the young man, trying to dig into him with its teeth. Every time the creature opened its mouth, Tahoe dropped a poison arrow down its throat. The creature was defeated, and soon it fell deep into the lake and drowned.

Watching from the shore, the young woman was devastated. She believed the man she

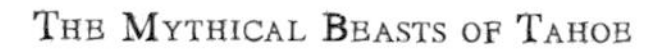

loved had died. She jumped into her canoe and rowed out to the place where the creature had crashed into the water.

"Oh, Tahoe, my love!" she said, falling into despair.

But suddenly, her sorrow turned to joy: There was Tahoe, standing on the giant bird's wing. He had survived! Now there was no question. He was *definitely* the bravest man around. The two were soon married and lived peacefully forever after. In honor of Tahoe's bravery against the Ong, the lake was named after him.

Isn't it nice, for a change, to have a monster story with a happy ending?

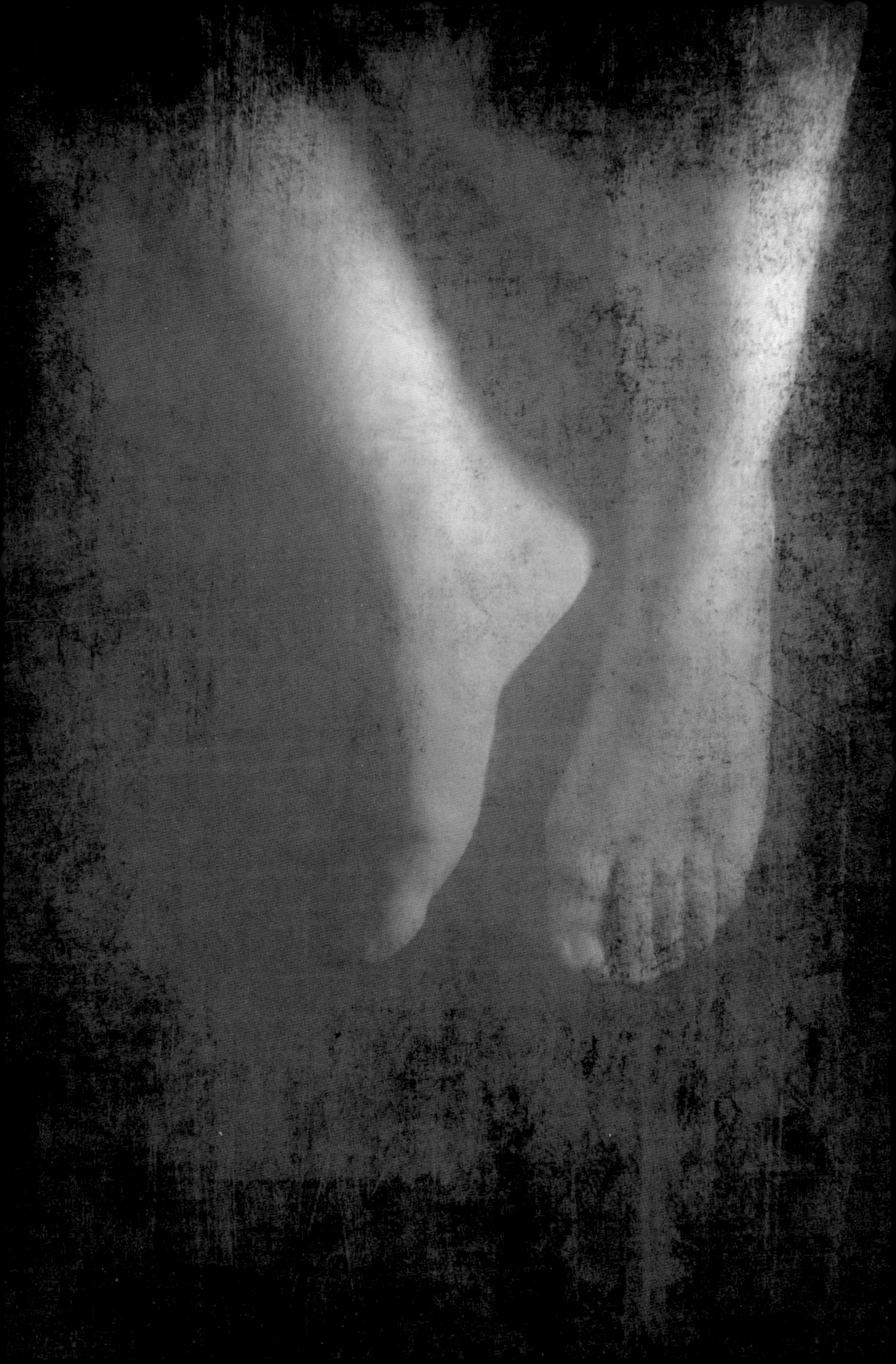

The Lake Never Gives Up Its Dead

As you can already tell, there's something very mysterious about the waters of Lake Tahoe. Through the years, some unfortunate souls have disappeared into the lake and never returned. Some say the waters keep them trapped within its depths. As far back as the 1870s, a local reporter explained that the high altitude makes the water here less dense.

That's why, he explained, those who drown here are never found.

Scientists now know it's the cold temperature that keeps bodies from decomposing and rising to the surface. There's long been a grisly rumor that when the famous oceanographer Jacques Cousteau explored the lake in a small, sub-like craft, he told the world it was not ready for the horrors that lay at the bottom of the lake.

In truth, it wasn't Cousteau who visited the lake, but his grandson. Still, the point behind the rumor is crystal clear. Many think the bottom of the lake is littered with corpses. People who have disappeared into the lake's mysterious depths, never to be seen again. If that's true, it would certainly explain why there are so many ghosts haunting Tahoe's shores.

For generations, locals have shared stories of strange happenings and eerie specters.

Perhaps the restless spirits of Indigenous peoples. Boaters and swimmers who have drowned. Laborers who helped build the railroad across the Sierra Nevada Mountains in the 1860s. Even Las Vegas mobsters who got themselves *deep*, shall we say, trouble.

On the California side of the lake, people often see the ghost of a little girl known as the Sugar Pine Point ghost. According to the local story, when she was around eleven or twelve, the girl and her family were guests of the Hellman family, the owners of the Hellman-Ehrman mansion, built in 1903. It's now part of Sugar Pine Point State Park.

One day, the families went out for a picnic. Everyone was on the beach when a few of the children slipped away to swim, including the little girl. When she disappeared, none of her friends noticed. When the rest of the children returned to the beach, they finally realized she wasn't with them. As the day wore on, she never returned.

For over a week, search parties looked for the little girl, but she was never found. Today, some say they see her on the shore. She is said to have long, straight blonde hair, and often wears a light blue dress with a big white collar—the exact kind worn by girls her age around the turn of the twentieth century. Those who have seen her say she appears around sunset and looks very sad. Do you think she's scared and lonely, perhaps?

Well, maybe not so lonely. After all, the little girl may not be alone at Sugar Pine Point. She might enjoy the company of San Francisco businessman I.W. Hellman—the man who hosted her family on that fateful day—whose spirit also never left the property. Many say his ghost continues to haunt the mansion to this day.

But these are just a few of Lake Tahoe's ghostly secrets.

Back in 1994, the lake claimed another soul. Scuba diving is a popular activity at the lake. A couple of friends went diving and, at first, all was going well. But just as one of the friends was about to resurface, something went wrong. Without any warning, he suddenly began to sink. His friends quickly called for help and rescue teams set out to look for him, hoping to reach him in time. But to everyone's horror, the diver was nowhere to be found. Hours and hours of searching returned the same result: there was no trace of the diver anywhere.

For years, his disappearance into the lake's chilly depths remained a mystery. But then, almost exactly seventeen years from the day he had disappeared, his body was found, still perfectly preserved in his scuba gear, wearing his tank.

Mysterious, indeed.

(Not to mention spooky.)

Another ghostly tale involves Captain Barter. *What happened to him?* you might ask.

The old sailor was known around the lake as the "Hermit of Emerald Bay." (Emerald Bay is considered one of Lake Tahoe's most beautiful locations and is famous for its mountain views, sandy beaches, and shimmering blue-green water.) The captain worked as a caretaker at the Holladay Estate. But when he was off duty, he frequented the saloons across the shores, rowing to them on his old boat, the *Nancy*. He kept the patrons riveted with his wild stories. One night, he calmly told everyone what happened when he'd been caught in a winter storm and his toes froze: he cut them off himself with a butcher knife and kept them! Captain Barter was famous for showing off his toes to visitors as proof that his story was true. This wasn't his only quirky behavior, if you can believe it.

Captain Barter built himself a memorial crypt on the top of a small uninhabited island so that when he died, he'd have a proper place to spend eternity. One stormy night in 1873, Captain Barter's luck ran out. As he left a saloon, he scanned the sky and spotted a storm brewing on the horizon. He had made it through rough weather before, though, so he decided to test his luck. He got in his rowboat and set out across the lake for Emerald Bay. He had almost made it back when a giant wave capsized the *Nancy* and broke her completely apart.

Captain Barter was a strong swimmer, so he must have thought he could make it safely back to shore. But the next day, the broken timbers of the *Nancy* were found floating off Rubicon Point.

Captain Barter's body was never found.

After all that work building the crypt, he was never laid to rest there. Later, the crypt was destroyed so that a tea house could be built in its place for the estate of a wealthy woman.

Maybe that's why some people claim to have seen Captain Barter's ghost walking along the lonely shore on foggy mornings and evenings. Alas, his restless spirt has nowhere to go.

The Ghostly Thunderbird Lodge

Coming around the rocky Eastern shore of Lake Tahoe, you see it: a storybook brick house with a slanted roof. You've arrived at Thunderbird Lodge. It looks like the kind of enchanted cottage you'd find in a fairytale forest. But is it enchanted . . . or haunted?

A wealthy California man named George Whittell, Jr. built the lodge in 1936. Whittell wanted a summer home on his Lake Tahoe property. He hired a famous architect to design it so that it would blend in perfectly with the natural beauty of the lake. Once it was done, he entertained many celebrity guests here. His parties were the talk of the town. He played loud music on his phonograph (an old-fashioned record player) and turned it up even louder when his neighbors complained. He even had a pet lion that was said to freely roam around the grounds! Just think how you might feel about hanging out with a lion. *No thanks!*

Whittell, who also went by the nickname "The Captain," had several additional structures built on the property. One was called the Card House because guests played games there. It was almost a private casino. There was an underground tunnel running

from the main house to the Card House. People said The Captain would lock guests in a little jail cell along the tunnel if their behavior got out of hand during his wild parties.

When he grew older, The Captain socialized less and less frequently. In the 1950s, his girlfriend died in a car accident. The Captain had her wrecked car brought back to the lodge. People said he would go to the car each day so that he could talk to his girlfriend's ghost. Rumors swirled that he would even have his servants play funeral music on repeat while he stood at the crunched-up car.

But then the stories coming out of Thunderbird Lodge got even stranger. When the pool house was being renovated, one of the workmen fell off a ladder to his death. The Captain ordered that the room be sealed up immediately. Even the ladder was left at the bottom of the pool.

When The Captain died in 1969, his estate was sold. Today, it is open to the public from May until mid-October. But be warned: If you happen to visit, you may run into a ghost. Or at the very least, you may experience something *ghostly*.

Inside the house, items move as if by an invisible hand. Around the grounds, people report many eerie happenings—especially at the pool house, which has reopened. It's said to possess a spooky feeling. Could it be the workman, still haunting the place where he took his tragic fall? Possibly, but he may not be the only ghost there, if you can believe it.

Psychic investigators visiting the Card House and the boathouse said they felt unexpected chills in the air. Then, they saw a shadowy woman fall over the side of the rocky cliff and down the shore—only to find out there the was no one there.

One paranormal investigation team brought recording equipment to capture ghostly sounds. When they played back the recording, they heard mysterious chanting and drumming. Perhaps it was echoes of songs of the Washoe people who once lived on the lake's shores? Others, meanwhile, heard something far more sinister: they claimed to have heard cries for help on the recording.

The lodge's gift shop was once the maid's and butler's living quarters. Now, it's said to be *very* haunted. There are unexplained cold spots and drafts. And what about that tunnel linking the main house to the Card House? Paranormal investigators went to check it out. Immediately, several in the group felt something unseen rushing past them. Two of them were so afraid, they started to run as eerie whispers began to echo through the tunnel.

But where did the whispers come from?

It's possible they simply got spooked hearing people in the nearby Card Room talking. But one psychic was *certain* there was a spirit in the tunnel. Later, he figured out that the rushing presence some of them felt must have been the ghost of the Captain's lion. As if a lion wasn't frightening enough in real life—a lion from the *afterlife* would be sure to send shivers down the spine!

Some believe the Captain's ghost still haunts the lodge. (Maybe his beloved girlfriend's ghost is there, too.) One paranormal hunter claimed his equipment detected the sounds of two spirits arguing—a male and female voice. Could the ghostly duo have been the Captain and his girlfriend, locked in an eternal lover's quarrel? Of course, anything is possible.

When another ghost hunting team from the United Kingdom arrived to investigate, one of the investigators saw a picture of the

Captain on the wall. She pointed to it and said, "I don't like this man. He was not a nice person." Not long after, while looking around the boathouse, the ghost hunter was attacked by an unseen force.

(I guess the Captain wasn't a fan of the investigator, either!)

In one of the upstairs bedrooms, another psychic investigator witnessed a woman crying. But no one else was on that floor of the house at the time. When she and the rest of the team returned to the room, one of the psychics asked the ghost several questions. They never heard an answer, and it's quite possible that no one ever will.

When it comes to the Thunderbird Lodge, nothing is for certain.

Spooky Shores and Summits

Tahoe's rocky shores are part of what make it so beautiful. But they can also be deadly. Have you ever heard of Shakespeare Rock? It's a dramatic rock formation on Tahoe's northeast shore that offers a beautiful view over the lake. Lots of locals and tourists like to hike there for picnics. It's a perfect way to spend an afternoon.

At least, for *most* people.

For the hikers who set out to the rock one day in 1877, a pleasant afternoon became a nightmare.

It was a fine fall day when a group of friends left Carson City, Nevada, for a day of sightseeing near the lake. Two members of the group were teenagers Carrie Rice and William Cramer. The friends stopped to gaze out at the beautiful view. While some of their friends stayed back from the edge of the rock, William and Carrie proceeded down a narrow path, holding hands. Neither of the teens were

wearing proper hiking shoes. As they stepped onto a loose bit of the trail, the ground began to give way beneath them. They started to slide down the cliff. The pair clasped at each other, trying to find something to hold on to. Their horrified friends looked on, unable to do anything. They heard Carrie say, "William, we are to die!"

Just as all hope was about to be lost, William succeeded in grabbing a tree root. But Carrie was not so lucky. She tumbled over the edge and fell to her death. Those who visit the area now say they can still hear her sobs in the spot where Carrie took her last breath. Others say it's just the wind through the trees. Maybe you should visit Shakespeare Rock and decide for yourself. But if you do, be careful. Carrie and William found out firsthand how dangerous the area can be.

Few people see the higher peaks of the Sierras. Only experienced hikers can make the trek. But if you're a passenger on the California Zephyr train, you roll right through the difficult terrain on tracks first laid in the 1860s. The construction of this railroad track took six years. It was dangerous work in a rugged environment. Most of the work was completed by Chinese immigrants who had come to the United States in search of a better life. Sadly, many of them did not find it here. Their lives ended by the side of these tracks.

Now, on clear winter nights, train passengers look out the windows and see ghostly figures in long white robes. They have a sad, solemn presence, and all seem to be pointing in the same direction. Are they trying to show the living the place where their lives ended? Additionally, some believe these ghosts might be the victims of a horrible train crash that happened here in 1868 during a blinding snowstorm.

The snowy peaks were also the scene of another terrible accident.

In March 1964, a plane on its way to Tahoe Valley Airport didn't make it. A late winter storm with heavy snow resulted in zero visibility. The plane slammed into Genoa Peak, leaving no survivors. Efforts to retrieve the victims took weeks since the desolate area is hard for rescuers to reach. But, those who do visit now describe an unsettling atmosphere, as if they can feel the tragedy still hanging in the air.

Another restless spirit suffered in a catastrophe nearby. A certain Mr. Childers haunts the area around Glenbrook, where he once owned a store. He came to Tahoe in 1874, hoping to take advantage of the local timber boom. He got into business with J.A. Rigby and the two had a successful general store that sold just about everything new settlers to the area needed.

But one day, Mr. Childers disappeared without a trace. No note. No goodbyes. He didn't even give notice to his business partner, Mr. Rigby. What could have happened? A search party went out to look for him, but days passed and neither the man nor his remains were ever found.

Nonetheless, time moved on, and J.A. Rigby decided to get on with his life. He found two new business partners and changed the name of the store. But three years later, the store burned to the ground. Some believe that

Childers's spirit was offended that his business partner had forgotten him and moved on so quickly. Is it possible Childers burned down Rigby's store in an act of revenge?

Some people in these parts think he did.

If you visit, be sure to ask the locals what they know about the legend of the scorned businessman. And stay on your toes in case you happen to run into a rather *grumpy* ghost . . .

CHAPTER 5

Celebrity Ghosts at the Cal Neva

If you're staying at a hotel near Lake Tahoe, chances are your hotel is haunted—because so many of them are! In fact, there are so many hotel ghosts in and around Lake Tahoe, it would be a surprise if the hotel you stay at didn't have one.

Unfortunately, you won't be able to stay at the lake's *most* haunted hotel, the Cal Neva Lodge on Crystal Bay. That's because it's now closed permanently. Could it have been just TOO haunted?

Built in 1926, the Cal Neva was a famous getaway for silent film stars. Situated on a bluff with stunning panoramic views, some people even called it the Queen of Lake Tahoe. Some of the biggest Hollywood stars were guests here, including Judy Garland (who played Dorothy in *The Wizard of Oz*).

When the singer Frank Sinatra bought the hotel in the 1960s, it became an even more popular destination. Sinatra invited his many famous friends to stay—and he had a lot of them! Singers like Dean Martin and Sammy Davis Jr., the famous actor and vaudeville performer Will Rogers, and American baseball legend Joe DiMaggio. He even built a heliport on the property for those who would fly to the resort in private helicopters. One of Sinatra's famous friends was Marilyn Monroe, the time's most sought-after actress in the world. Some say that these two major celebrities never checked out of the Cal Neva.

Monroe stayed in a cabin at the hotel shortly before she died. There have been sightings of her in the cabin and throughout the Cal Neva property—in the main lodge, the tunnel, and at the pool. One guest in the main lodge claimed she felt Marilyn in the room with her. Just moments later, her husband felt something brush against his neck and bump his head!

Did Marilyn's ghost *really* return to this beloved Tahoe retreat to stay forever? Ghost hunters have visited Marilyn's cabin to try to contact her from beyond the grave. They brought dowsing rods (a kind of tool used to pick up sensitive vibrations from the earth), cameras, and special ghost-hunting audio recorders. Several ghost hunters believed that Marilyn *was* there— and that she was dancing!

The Cal Neva also had a very special pool. It was said to be the only one in the entire United States that crossed state lines. In fact, the state border was actually painted on the bottom. So if you swam back and forth across the pool, you'd go from California to Nevada and back again.

(Now that's one big pool!)

One guest was in the pool when he swore he saw Marilyn Monroe's ghost swimming next to him. He said she swam from one side of the pool to the other, grabbed the railing on the steps, and then vanished into the night.

Frank Sinatra's ghost, on the other hand, is believed to stay mostly inside his cabin. But ghost hunters and employees alike have sensed his presence in the lodge, too. One employee was alone in the showroom and decided to sing a Sinatra song.

Although no one was with her, she felt a hand placed heavily on her shoulder. Immediately, the employee got the sense that it was Frank's ghost—and he *didn't* want her singing his song. Other employees have reported hearing laughter or piano music echoing from the showroom when no one is there.

Cal Neva employees say that Frank's ghost doesn't like it when people make jokes about him. One day, when a musical group was rehearsing, a member of the group made a joke about the lodge's ghosts. The words were barely out of his mouth when the band's equipment suddenly stopped working.

Talk about a real showstopper!

That wasn't the only time Frank's ghost got a little fresh. Ghost hunters who came to find Frank were shocked when one of their remote controls rose in the air and turned around before coming back to rest on the desk. One even felt a hand on her leg when there was no one around.

Frank seems to enjoy messing around in the light booth, too. Those who work there say that when the room is locked, items mysteriously move or go missing. One employee said that each time he left and turned out the lights, he'd return to find them back on, even though the room was still locked and no one else had been inside. Another employee said she saw a heavy door, which could barely be budged, swing wide open on its own and then slam shut with a bang.

The third most spotted ghost at the Cal Neva is Sam Giancana, a famous gangster. The story goes that Sam spent a lot of time at the lodge—especially backstage—as he waited for his girlfriend, a professional dancer, to finish her shows. One psychic investigating the area felt the presence of a ghost. She said it was "someone who hadn't been very nice in life—someone a little rough around the edges." That certainly sounds like it could have been a gangster, but it also could have been one of Sam's bodyguards, who were often with him.

All three of the Cal Neva's famous ghosts have been sensed in the tunnel that ran underground between the main lodge and some of the private cabins. During the Prohibition period in the 1920s and early 1930s, alcohol and gambling were illegal in the United States. The tunnel at the Cal Neva helped owners and patrons of the hotel carry on drinking and gambling without law enforcement finding out. Later, celebrities and politicians who wanted a little privacy from the paparazzi used the tunnel to sneak around the property.

Out of sight, out of mind.

These days, it's still easy to hide in the tunnel—especially if you're a ghost. Those who've walked it say there are unexplained cold spots. Some have reported feeling something (or someone) unseen brush past them. Ghost hunters sense many spirits in the tunnel, yet they haven't seen any apparitions—only glowing orbs. Could these mysterious balls of light be the spirits of Marilyn or Frank? Or perhaps they are less famous spirts from Prohibition days, still up to their old tricks . . . and still on the run from the law.

Not surprisingly, the Cal Neva was more than just a hotel. It was also a casino. According to past employees, some *very* strange things happened in the "pit," the area where the blackjack tables were arranged in a circle. Blackjack is a card game in which a dealer stands behind the table and deals cards while the players stand in front. A "pit boss" walks around to ensure that no one is cheating.

One time, a ghost hunter was in the

casino and briefly saw a group of people near a blackjack table. They looked like they had stepped out of the 1940s. Were they just tourists dressing up for fun? It looked like they were having a good time. The ghost hunter observed them laughing and talking, although she couldn't hear what they were saying. When she got to the table, she asked the dealer who the guests were. But he didn't seem to know what she was talking about. When she looked up again, they had disappeared. That night, every time she walked past the table, she saw the people again. But no one else saw them. In the end, she decided they must be *time-warp ghosts*—a kind of spirit who is unaware they are visible to a person in a future time.

Will the Cal Neva ever reopen its doors? Right now, it's not certain. The living may not be able to go in . . . but the ghostly spirts sure do have the time of their afterlives stepping out!

Two Ghosts Named Mary

Is there something particularly spooky about the name Mary? Not really, but it just so happens that two of Tahoe's most famous ghosts share the name and both live in hotels. It's probably just a coincidence, *right*?

Our first ghostly Mary lives in the Rainbow Lodge on the Yuba River. The current hotel was built over an old stagecoach stop on the Emigrant Trail—the path settlers took on their way to California. It was constructed in the early 1900s and expanded through the years. During the middle of the twentieth century, it became a fancy destination for skiers. Now, it's a place where weddings and family reunions take place.

Since it's been around so long, it's no wonder the Rainbow Lodge is believed to house so many ghosts, such as the gambler often spotted in the dining room. But the one everyone talks about is known as Mary.

Who was she in life? No one is completely sure, but there are a few theories. Some say her husband killed her in a jealous rage after finding her with another man. Others say she was never with someone else—though her husband mistakenly thought she was. Whatever the reason, Mary has never completely checked out of Room 23. Guests have mentioned the lights flickering on and off on their own, and the unpleasant sensation of having their arms pinched. In other locations around the hotel, people have reported hearing a woman weeping.

However, at least one guest has taken a photo of Mary. She appears as a smoky outline of a woman. Of course, it depends on who you ask. Others just see a blur in the photo!

Our second Mary is a little easier to see. She lives at the Tahoe Biltmore, one of the first casinos built on the shores of Lake Tahoe. The casino was once reserved for the rich and famous, who visited to gamble and enjoy entertainment. Now, everyone is welcome.

The name of the hotel was changed to the Nevada Lodge and then changed back to the Tahoe Biltmore again. The hotel's permanent resident is

known by the nickname Biltmore Mary. She's such an important part of the hotel that new employees learn all about her.

Mary was one of the dancers who entertained casino guests back when the hotel was known as the Nevada Lodge. The story goes that on a rainy night, Mary fought with her boyfriend, who was visiting her at work. It's said that she wanted to get married, and he didn't. Witnesses saw him storm out of the casino. Brokenhearted, Mary stayed in the bar, drinking and crying. No one is quite sure what happened next. Some say she was so distressed, she took her own life in her hotel room. Others say that in her grief, she drove too fast down the winding road leaving the hotel and crashed.

Although it's not certain how she passed away, those who work at the Tahoe Biltmore mostly agree that Mary is still there. The hotel has a wedding chapel, and Mary is known for hanging around there. Her presence is easy to sense, like a cold breeze in the air. She flicks the lights on and off, and sometimes moves things around backstage in the showroom, where she spent some of her happiest hours.

One employee didn't believe the stories of Mary's ghost until one winter night when the casino was nearly empty. He went outside to check on the snow coming down. When he went back inside, he felt a sharp chill in the air—even though he'd shut the door behind him. He looked around, suddenly feeling as if he was being watched. The employee shook the feeling off. He told himself to stop being silly.

But as he walked down the hall, the same eerie feeling crept back over him. He spun around quickly to see who was behind him, but no one was there. Heart racing, he took one more step.

And that's when he heard it.

The sound of a woman laughing.

Officially frightened, the man ran into the hotel's showroom, the place where the dancers used to entertain guests. The laughter returned, but this time it was louder. That's when he felt a chill wrap around him. His whole body turned cold! He tried to tell himself it was all his imagination—but just as he started to

calm down, he felt a tap on his shoulder! Again, he turned. *And again*, no one was there!

In an instant, all the stories he had heard about Mary came rushing back. It must be her.

"I know you're here, Mary," he said, eyes darting around the room. Nobody answered him and he never encountered her again. But the man knew, without a doubt, it had been her.

Did she just need someone to acknowledge her presence?

Maybe.

After all, even ghosts need a little attention sometimes.

Years later, another manager at the Tahoe Biltmore heard the story of Mary—and she too was skeptical. Every time something went missing or was out of place at the hotel, her coworkers would blame the ghost.

"Mary took my phone."

"Mary lost the paperwork."

Okay, the manger thought. *Right*.

She knew *she* would never blame a ghost for a mistake she'd made. After all, the manager was super-organized and very tidy. Things like that didn't happen to her.

Until one day.

A coworker lost an important file and blamed it, as usual, on Mary. The manager snapped. "Why do you keep blaming a *phantom*?" she demanded. "Take some responsibility for your actions!"

But her coworker was positive she hadn't lost the file. "I set it right there on the desk. And now it's gone!"

The manager shook her head and said, "I'm tired of hearing about Mary."

The next morning when the manager came into work, she was shocked to discover that her desk was a mess. Papers were scattered all over the place. She knew no one had been in the room since she had locked it the night before. That’s when she, like the manager years before her, heard the faraway sound of a woman laughing. A sudden chill came over her as she realized Mary had gotten her revenge.

All right, Mary,” she said. “I believe you’re here. But please don’t mess with my stuff again. *Please?*”

For what it’s worth, Mary honored the manager’s wish from that day forward.

Haunted Highways

Have you ever taken a ride around the north shore of Lake Tahoe? If you have, you were probably on Route 28. It is a road with amazing, pristine views of the lake and the mountains, perfect for an afternoon drive. The sights are unforgettable, but this road is also sometimes treacherous. In the fog, snow, or heavy rain, it can be very difficult for drivers to see into the distance. There are many sharp turns. And late at night, there are few streetlights to chase away the dark. In the near pitch blackness, the shadows on the side of the road might not seem so harmless. You might even think you see something. Or *someone*. You wouldn't be the first. More than one ghost is believed to haunt this stretch of road.

Drivers have reported seeing a man who looks confused standing on the side of the road. Imagine *their* confusion when they do a double take and find that he's gone.

Locals know him as The Ghost of Highway 28. In fact, he's been seen so many times over the years, he's practically a local himself. Some think he's the ghost of Richard Anderson, a sheriff's deputy who died on the road in 1962. He's rumored to have a connection to another ghost in this book. Or shall we say, the man who later *became* that ghost: Frank Sinatra.

The story goes that Anderson's wife worked

as a waitress at the Cal Neva. Yes, the very same hotel and casino featured in a previous story. She caught the eye of Frank Sinatra, who was disappointed to learn she was already married. But husband or not, whenever he saw her, he'd flirt with her. When the woman told her husband Richard about this, he was angry. One night when he was picking her up from work, he confronted Sinatra and told him to leave his wife alone. Although Sinatra was often known to pick a fight, this time he only apologized and said he would stop. It may sound like this story is headed for a happy ending, but it took a different turn.

According to rumors, a week later, Sinatra saw Anderson at the hotel. This time he *did* pick a fight. But he chose the wrong person to fight with: Anderson was much bigger than Sinatra. He punched Sinatra in the face. With an injured nose, Sinatra couldn't perform at Cal Neva's show room. That made him even angrier.

Now, the two were enemies.

If the story is true, the rivalry came to a deadly end two weeks later, on July 17, 1962. Anderson was driving on Route 28 with his wife in the passenger seat. It's said that a big maroon convertible came up behind them and forced their car off the road. Anderson swerved and lost control of the car. He hit a tree and was killed instantly. His wife was thrown from the car and injured. Meanwhile, the driver of the convertible sped away.

Who was the driver? Some thought it was a drunk driver who didn't want to get caught. Others thought it was someone showing off in their fancy car. But there was a more sinister rumor. What if

Sinatra had sent someone to knock Anderson off the road? That's what Anderson's parents thought. We may never know if that ghostly man often seen on this stretch of road is his spirit, but plenty of people believe it could be.

Over on Highway 50 in El Dorado National Forest, there's another roadside ghost with an even stranger tale. It was the summer of 1994 when a woman was driving on a lonely stretch of Highway 50 close to Bullion Bend. It was so dark that she couldn't see well. Besides the trees, there wasn't much to see. Until the driver noticed something odd.

Very odd.

She saw a woman on the side of the road without a stitch of clothing on. Even stranger—the roadside woman seemed to be glowing in the darkness! The driver was terrified. Instead of stopping, she decided to go straight to the sheriff's office to report what she saw. The officers said they'd check it out immediately. But when they got there, there was no one in sight.

The next morning, the police returned to check out the scene again, hoping maybe they had missed something in the dark. They *had*.

First, they found a child's shoe. Could this belong to the child who, with his mother, had been missing from nearby Placerville for three days? The mother had told her friends that she and her son were headed in that direction. But they never arrived at their destination.

There were no skid marks nor any other indication of a wreck on the road. But then, a deputy looked down over the cliffside. Although it was mostly hidden, he spotted a car that had tumbled over the side of the cliff and landed forty feet down. Inside it, rescuers found the three-year-old boy, miraculously still alive. But sadly, his mother had died behind the wheel.

Had the mother's ghost climbed the ravine to the side of the road to alert passersby to the crash? That's what some think. If that's true, the mother's ghost saved her son's life. Maybe the woman driving past had seen a guardian angel? Or perhaps she'd just imagined the woman on the side of the road. It would certainly be a strange coincidence.

Whatever really happened that night, the incident is so remarkable, and so hard to believe, that it's become one of Tahoe's most talked-about ghost stories.

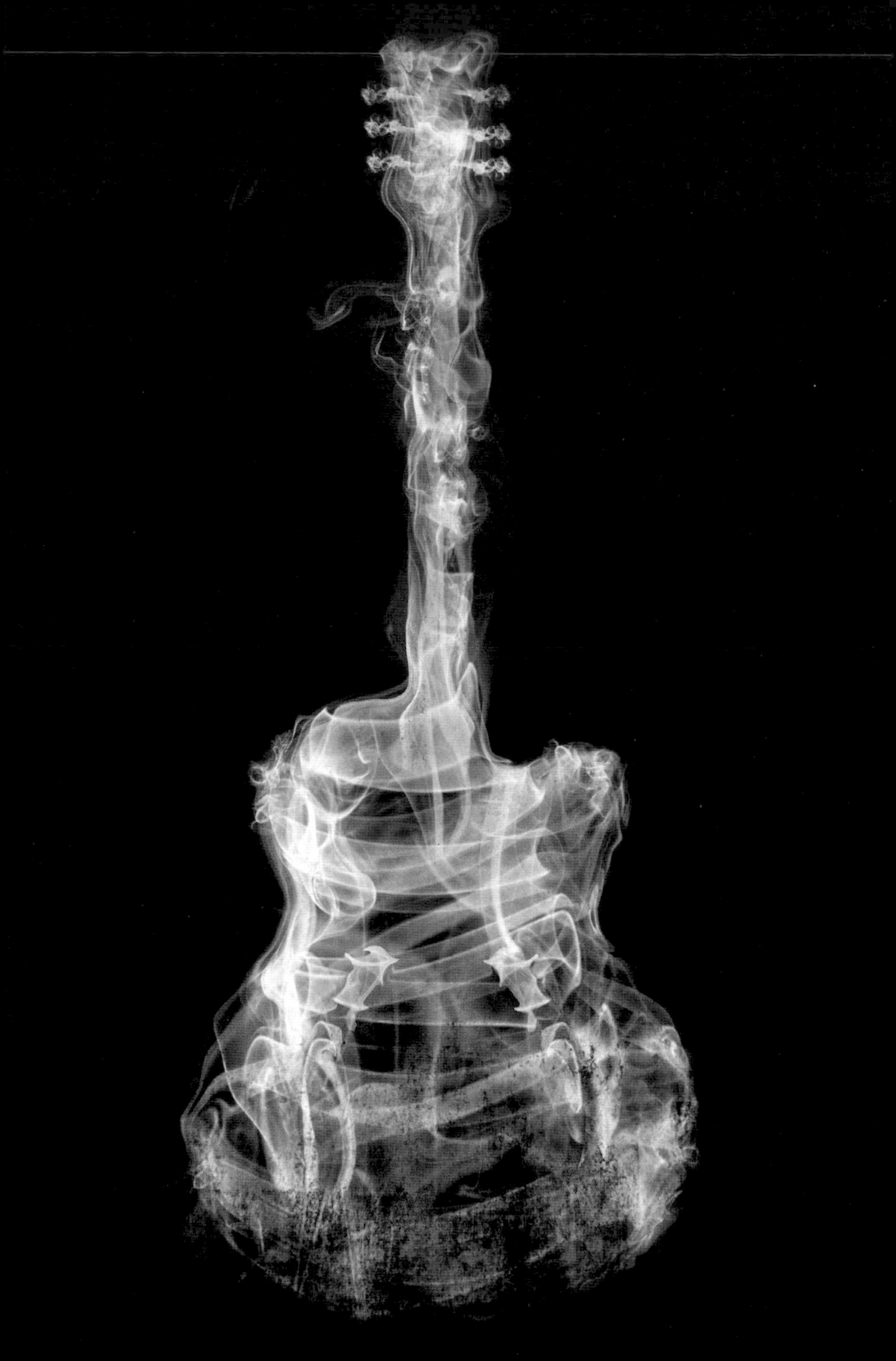

Hard Rock Hauntings

You're not tired of haunted hotels yet, are you?

Good.

Because there's another one you need to know about.

Around Lake Tahoe, it's not unusual for a hotel to change owners and names many times through the years. Take the Hard Rock Hotel, for example. That's the name now, but the hotel has had different names in the past.

It was the Sahara and the Horizon Hotel not long ago. Each time the hotel changes owners, it gets lots of updates. Teams of electricians, carpenters, and other remodeling experts come in to make the changes. But at the Hard Rock, there are places construction crews just don't like to spend time.

There is a small tower at the back of the hotel, for example. It seems like ghosts there don't like the remodeling because they play all kinds of tricks on the workers. In fact, some ghost hunters say the best way to get a ghost to show up is to start a remodeling project. We may not know much about the supernatural world, but we *do* know one thing: ghosts don't like change.

There's a very spooky story about something that happened in the hotel's casino one night. A security guard got a call from the hotel's dispatcher. "You've got to go down to the pit right away," she told the guard. "There might be some kids messing around in there."

The security guard wasn't worried. After all, strange things happen in casinos, and she was pretty sure she'd seen it all by that point.

The guard arrived in the casino. To her surprise, she immediately felt the hair on her neck stand up. She looked around, sensing something she couldn't explain. In addition to the blackjack tables, the room housed the hotel's amazing stage. When a big act or performer had a show, the stage would rise out of the pit and into the showroom upstairs so that the performer could make a very dramatic entrance. A cement barrier surrounded the stage. The guard realized as she walked around that it was kind of a dangerous situation. A person could fall through the opening around the stage if they were not careful.

The security guard started to worry. Had someone fallen into the opening between the stage and the barrier and gotten trapped? She walked past the dressing room and suddenly heard something unexpected. It was a strange sound, like someone was . . . dragging something. A piece of cloth, or maybe plastic?

The guard frowned. Was something stuck to the bottom of her shoe? She stopped to check, but saw nothing. But then she realized the sound stopped when she stopped. "Hello?" she called out. But only the silence echoed back. Looking around the empty casino, the guard couldn't shake the eerie feeling that she was not alone. She walked to the stage once more, and the sound not only returned, but grew *louder*.

What IS that?

Heart pounding, the guard quickened her pace. When she sped up, the sound sped up.

She started to run.

Suddenly, it felt like the noise was right on top of her. But when she turned to look, there was nothing there. As quickly as she could, she raced back up the stairs to find the dispatcher.

"Well? Did you find those kids?" the dispatcher asked.

"No," the guard said. "But it was the craziest thing. It sounded like someone was *dragging* something across the floor. I'm not sure what it was. It was the strangest sound!"

"Do you know this hotel used to be the Sahara?" the dispatcher asked after a moment.

The guard shook her head. She didn't understand why that was important.

The dispatcher went on to explain. "Elvis used to perform here."

"Elvis Presley?" the guard said. "The King of Rock and Roll?" She knew some of his big songs like "Blue Suede Shoes" and "Hound

Dog." But she still didn't know why it mattered.

What the dispatcher said next left the guard speechless.

Apparently, the Sahara had *quite* a famous ghost on its hands.

"That sound you heard," the dispatcher said. "That was Elvis's *cape* dragging across the floor. He thought you were escorting him to the stage. When you stopped, he stopped. When you ran, *he* ran." The dispatcher explained that during a certain time of his life, Elvis was known to wear very heavy, elaborate capes when he performed. They were covered in plastic jewels and beads. No wonder it made such a distinctive noise when he dragged it across the floor!

It turned out the guard wasn't the first person to have unknowingly escorted Elvis. The hotel's maintenance men had reported the exact same experience many times. In fact, the King's ghost was a regular presence on the hotel's seventh floor, and employees there had seen him so often they barely took any notice of him!

What do you think? Would *you* ever want to escort the ghostly King of Rock and Roll? Or would you run away . . . howling like a hound dog?

Historic Downtown Truckee

Terrified in Truckee

There's far more to the Tahoe area than just water sports and hiking at the lake. Located between the outdoor paradise in Tahoe and the casinos in Reno, there's a little town where you can imagine what life might have been like during frontier times. Charming, historic Truckee gives you a sense of the real Wild West in the early days of California, when prospectors came from all over the world to try to look for gold and silver, then cash in on the booms in timber and mining. There's an old jail, a cemetery, historic train depot, and lots of original Victorian-era houses and buildings in town. With so much colorful history, is it any wonder that Truckee is so haunted?

For those coming west along the Emigrant Trail, Truckee was often the first stop in the California territory. The local Paiute people, who had been there for centuries, welcomed them. This new frontier town was named after their leader, who had long been a guide for explorers and settlers coming to the area. The first buildings of Truckee started out as a wagon road station in the 1860s. Timber and mining operations started up, and soon after, Truckee got its first railroad stop in 1868. Settlers looking to make their fortunes flocked to the town.

But not long after, the ghosts moved in, too.

In 1873, the local newspaper printed a story about a haunted house in town. The owners heard the ghosts of crying children coming from under the floorboards. The children begged for bread and shouted that they were afraid they would be taken from their parents. In one bedroom, an occupant was woken in the middle of the night by a giant man carrying a tin lantern. That would be scary enough, but the giant ghost threw his icy arms around the man and pinned him to the floor! With his one free arm, the man reached for his gun, which was laying on a chair near the bed. He managed to fire it off, but of course, bullets were useless because his attacker was a ghost.

The gunshot and shouts alerted the man's friend, whose bedroom in a neighboring house shared a wall with the haunted room. The friend arrived to help. The ghost had disappeared, but the man was still on the floor, frozen in terror. Not only that, but the room was a mess. Chairs were overturned, the bed sheets were tangled, and there was even blood on the floor!

While the man recovered, the evil presence in the house never left. The whole family reported that they experienced "manifestations of a mysterious and unaccountable nature," such as more children weeping and furniture being tossed around. Finally, the family couldn't take it anymore and moved out. Today, no one knows the location of the haunted house, since this happened almost one hundred and fifty years ago. But we do know of another haunting that started on High Street in 1877.

A feud broke out between two men by the names of Charlton and Smith, who lived in the same house. While their wives got along, the two men didn't. Tempers flared, and one fight led to Charlton murdering Smith in the heat of an argument. Charlton was jailed for it, later taking his own life in his cell. Soon after, the two men's widows were troubled to find that Smith haunted the home they shared, "making hideous noises and causing them the greatest consternation" according to the local newspaper. The women had to move out, but it's uncertain if the ghost ever did.

Truckee's most famous haunted building is the oldest building on Commercial Row and the second oldest in town. The Capitol, now a theater and gallery, was built by William Hurd in 1870. Hurd operated a saloon on the first floor.

Along with all the settlers, Truckee attracted a good number of criminals. (This was the Wild West, after all.) The town had a reputation for robberies. You might not be too surprised to learn that there were a number of gunfights in Hurd's saloon back in the day.

One day in 1891, a constable named Jake Teeter got into a gun fight with a man named James Reed. The two were known enemies. Teeter is believed to have started the shootout that ended his life. Now both men are buried in the Truckee Cemetery, but Teeter is, shall we say, *restless*. His ghost has been seen around the Capitol building on numerous occasions.

Once the days of shoot-outs were over, the Capitol hosted many famous guests in its saloon, including movie stars Clark Gable, Buster Keaton, and Charlie Chaplin. Chaplin stayed near Truckee while filming *Gold Rush*, a famous silent movie. While there, it's said he had a romance with his co-star. Did Chaplin enjoy his time in Truckee so much that he never left? Some say they've seen him on the second floor stage of the Capitol.

The second floor of the Capitol was also where members of a secret vigilante justice organization met. They were called the 601, which some say referred to their mission—six feet under, zero trials, and one rope. If the group wanted someone to leave town, they would hang red ribbons where the person could see them as a warning. The message was clear—leave town or die. One of the people who didn't heed the warning was Carrie Pryor, also known as Spring Chicken. After she showed her dislike for the group, it's said the members went after her in 1874. The showdown ended in a shoot-out. A prominent local man named D.B Frink was killed in the melee, and he's believed to still haunt the Capitol's second floor.

Remember Constable Teeter, the restless ghost of the Capitol? His wife's spirit is restless, too! It's believed her ghost haunts the River Street Inn, which was built atop where the couple's home used to be. Mrs. Teeter has been seen in the hallways and basement of the home. Some have even heard her speak. "Where is Jacob?" she asks.

She doesn't know he is haunting another Truckee building.

Given Truckee's reputation as a tough town, it's not surprising it needed a really strong jail! The one built in 1875 had 32-inch-thick walls lined in steel. It once housed everyone from cattle rustlers to brawlers. Most inmates held here were dying to get out of the jail, but it seems that some never managed to leave. Is it a lawman or a bunch of outlaws that haunt the Old Truckee Jail?

Psychic investigators have felt the presence of a sad spirit there. Some women who were held in the jail said they felt ghostly hands grabbing at them. You can now visit the jail, which operates as a museum. If you do, be alert for spirits or strange happenings.

One of the oldest houses in town is the Richardson House, a Victorian cottage built in 1887. The home belonged to Warren Richardson, who had come to Truckee in the 1850s seeking gold but ended up making a fortune with the timber mill he and his brother owned. The house is now a vacation home. A very *haunted* vacation home.

Luckily, the ghosts of the Richardson House are friendly. One is believed to be the spirit of an old woman who was a friend of the Richardson family. One snowy day, she made a long and difficult journey to reach the family home. When she arrived, her friends greeted her graciously. She was so tired from travel that she decided to turn in early for bed and bid her hosts good night. The snow continued to fall as they all slept, surrounding the home in deep drifts. When their guest didn't come down for breakfast in the morning, the Richardsons decided not to disturb her. After all, she was exhausted from travel. When they finally rapped on her door at 10:00 a.m., they received no answer. After a few more tries, they opened the door to find her dead in the guest room's four-poster bed.

Some say they can still feel her spectral presence in the same room today, although she has been spotted in other parts of the house as well. The home's current owners think she is responsible for moving a brass urn that is usually found on a shelf. They've gone out and returned home to find it on the dining room table.

The old lady may not be to blame, though. It's also said two ghost children haunt the house. Former owners of the house once heard a noise in the middle of the night. When they awoke in the morning, they found that their Christmas tree had been tipped over and every ornament was broken. Could the ghost children have gotten into some mischief? It is believed they died in the house. Maybe they feel that if they can't have Christmas anymore, no one else should? Then again, it's possible they are simply hoping to be noticed.

Locals also speak of another ghostly woman in the house. She's believed to be Maggie Richardson, looking for her child who died. Perhaps the ghost children are trying to get her attention?

The Gateway section of town might be Truckee's *most* haunted neighborhood. Another old woman haunts a home there, going about her daily routine in a kitchen that was once hers many years before. Too bad for the new owners, she seems completely unaware they have moved in!

The Sad Tale of the Donner Party

Have you heard of the California Trail? It was one of the pathways the early settlers of the West took to the new territories of California and Oregon before they became states.

Starting in the 1840s, thousands of hopeful people left their lives behind and joined wagon trains headed westward to look for a better life. Families put all their belongings into covered wagons and set out on long and difficult journeys, leaving from places in the Midwest—such as St. Louis or Independence, Missouri, or Council Bluffs, Iowa. They joined other families and traveled together for protection because the journey was dangerous. There were attacks from thieves and those who didn't want settlers to take their land. There was extreme heat and cold and frightening storms. Often, there was not enough food. But many decided that the promise of a bright future in the West was worth the risk.

In the spring of 1846, one of those families who set out on this dangerous journey was the Donner family, headed by George and Tamsen Donner. They were parents to five daughters. They began the journey with some

of their relatives. Other families joined them along the way. Eventually, their group grew to include eighty-seven men, women, and children destined for California. This group later became known as the Donner Party.

The journey was easy at first. They made good time and had good weather. But about six weeks into the trip, they faced a growing number of challenges. An elderly woman died. One of the party's leaders killed a man and was kicked out by the others. But everything got much, much worse when they made the decision to take a short cut.

At one of the forts along the way, they met a man who told them there was a faster and easier way to get to California called the Hastings Cutoff. The stranger seemed certain this way would not be too hard and would save them time. But others at the fort discouraged them from taking the Hastings Cutoff, saying it was *not* a shortcut and *was* too dangerous. But the leaders of the Donner Party decided to take a chance on it.

The road took them over the Wasatch Range of the Rocky Mountains. These mountains can be challenging to cross even with modern roads and vehicles. Just imagine what it was like in a covered wagon! Wagon wheels broke on the rocky paths. Both people and animals suffered injuries along the way.

Soon, the Donner Party arrived at the Great Salt Lake Desert. Their horses were tired and sick, and many in the group also became sick, or they perished in accidents. There was another murder, too. The "short cut" had cost the group a lot of time, and the trip was coming

apart at the seams. They were now behind schedule and would not be able to get over the mountains before the winter snows began. But they decided to try, anyway.

As they reached what's now Reno, Nevada, they could see the beautiful Sierra Mountains in the distance. They decided to rest before starting this last, difficult part of the journey. It was late October when they started into the mountain pass leading to California. Not long after they began, a storm rolled in, bringing icy cold. Next, a blizzard arrived, so strong that the desperate travelers couldn't see in front of them. Eventually, one of the wheels on the lead wagon broke. As George Donner tried to repair the wheel, he cut his hand badly. He told the

others in the wagon train to continue without him and his family. They would stay where they were at Alder Creek until his hand healed. The family made temporary shelters to protect themselves from the storm.

The other wagons were only able to get six miles ahead before the storm got so bad that they were forced to stop. One family found an abandoned cabin for shelter. Another built a shelter against a large boulder. The families were able to make fires and huddle under blankets. But as the days wore on and the storm didn't let up, their food supplies started to run out.

At first, with little other option, the families boiled leather and drank the water as broth. They ate tree branches and their livestock. But soon, the hunger was too much to bear—they began to eat their pets. And when there was nothing left of the animals' bare bones, the Donner Party did the unthinkable: they ate the corpses of their dead companions. Can you think of another scene as horrifying as the hungry Donners left without a choice?

Well, it was not until the following spring that rescuers found them. But by then it was too late. Forty-one members of the party had died, including both George and Tamsen Donner.

The tragedy was never forgotten, as the story spread across the United States and even around the world. For later settlers traveling through the California and Oregon territories, the story of the Donner party became a cautionary tale. Even today, people shudder when they think of what the victims and survivors endured.

Today, those who perished are remembered at Donner Memorial State Park. There is a museum there, and a monument to the many pioneers who traveled great distances to settle in the West. Inside, you can learn more about the Donner's story, as well as the stories of many others who traveled west on the Emigrant Trail. There is now a public hiking trail where the Donner family camped at Alder Creek. Some say the family's ghosts still haunt the area. Late at night, people have reported seeing the ghost of Tamsen Donner walking the grounds of the museum. She sacrificed herself so her daughters would have enough to eat and live through the winter. Perhaps she is still looking out for them from another dimension.

Others have seen a man in settler's clothes near the

museum and at Alder Creek. Could it be George or his brother Jacob, still trying to find a way out of their terrible situation?

Not long ago, a group of ghost hunters decided to check out the haunting rumors. When paranormal investigators recently visited the museum, some in the group felt a strong presence near the wagon display.

When they reached the boulder where one family had sheltered, a psychic in the group reported that she heard horses. She told the group they were standing near an unmarked grave. They called out the names of those who had died to ask what had happened to them. When they checked their recording equipment later, they heard the faint sound of someone saying *"lies."*

What did it mean? Some have suggested that what we believe happened to the Donner Party may not be entirely true. Indeed, a man impersonating a Donner party member told many gruesome stories for years that made their way around the new California settlements. So, we may never know exactly

what happened during that terrible winter. But traces of the tragedy have left a mark on this place forever.

If you visit Donner Memorial State Park or hike the Donner Camp Trail, perhaps *you* may meet a shadowy figure from yesteryear. Either way, you will be moved by the great—and in some cases *gruesome*—sacrifices many made for a better life in a new land.

A Ghostly Goodbye

There's so much to explore at Lake Tahoe, from the rocky bays to the historic homes and hotels to the many hiking trails. It's a stunningly beautiful place that some people never want to leave.

And some never do.

While you're enjoying water sports—from stand-up paddleboarding to kayaking—have fun and make sure you're observing all safety precautions. Now you know that you might not *really* want to get a closer look at the bottom of the lake . . .

If you're driving late at night, stay alert for any roadside ghosts. And if you're vacationing in one of the many local lodges, be aware that every single one has its own story.

And even in an empty room, you may not really be alone.

In a place with as much history as Lake Tahoe, there are bound to be lingering spirits lurking about. But don't be frightened. Most of them are just lonely or looking for a little entertainment. Like Elvis, they might just want to enjoy your company.

Whoever you meet—and whatever realm they may be from—you will certainly have a memorable time at Lake Tahoe. And even if you don't have your own ghostly encounters, now you have some unforgettable spooky stories to share.

Kate Byrne grew up listening to stories about banshees, fairies, and ghosts in grand Irish houses. She loves hearing and telling spooky, supernatural stories and is always on the lookout for a good haunted house, a ghostly graveyard, and shape-shifting creatures.

Check out some of the other *Spooky America* titles available now!

Spooky America was adapted from the creeptastic *Haunted America* series for adults. *Haunted America* explores historical haunts in cities and regions across America. Here's more from the original *Haunted Lake Tahoe* author Janice Oberding: